THE ELECTION OMEN

10 DAY DEVOTIONAL

THE ELECTION OMEN
10 DAY DEVOTIONAL

Copyright © 2020 Marsha Kuhnley
Visit the author's website at Rapture911.com

All rights reserved. No part of the non-biblical text in this publication may be reproduced, distributed, or transmitted in any form or by any means, including photocopying, recording, or other electronic or mechanical methods, without the prior written permission of the publisher, except in the case of brief quotations embodied in critical reviews and certain other noncommercial uses permitted by copyright law.

The text of the World English Bible (WEBP) is in the public domain and may be copied freely.

Published by Drezhn Publishing LLC
PO BOX 67458
Albuquerque, NM 87193-7458

Cover Design by Drezhn Publishing LLC

Print Edition - April 2020
First Edition

ISBN 978-1-947328-42-6

Unless otherwise indicated, all Scripture quotations are taken from the World English Bible (WEBP), a public domain translation of the Holy Bible.

Scripture quotations marked (NLT) are taken from the Holy Bible, New Living Translation, copyright © 1996, 2004, 2015 by Tyndale House Foundation. Used by permission of Tyndale House Publishers, Inc., Carol Stream, Illinois 60188. All rights reserved.

THE ELECTION OMEN

10 DAY DEVOTIONAL

Marsha Kuhnley

INTRODUCTION

Jesus has entrusted each of us with his Great Commission. We're to go into the world and preach the gospel (Mark 16:15). Did you know that our nation's founders who sailed across the ocean on the Mayflower ship were fulfilling this God given mission? On Day 1, you're going to read about the mission they embarked on to bring God glory. It's the same mission you have too.

In the subsequent days, you're going to read the Declaration of Independence and President George Washington's Inaugural Address and discover how America was not only founded to bring God glory, but that it's the key to your life, liberty, and happiness.

In this devotional, each day you'll read one of the historical founding documents of the United States and a selection of Scripture that I've chosen that illustrates the biblical truths corresponding to the topic of the day. I've underlined some of the text in the historical documents so you can easily refer back to statements we're focusing on each day.

The daily reading is followed up by a brief explanation of the Scripture. Then comes the lesson and application in which I present you a key truth and a question to consider for the day. The daily reading ends with a prayer. I estimate it'll take you about ten minutes to read each day.

Get ready to see God's plan for America and for you revealed!

THE MAYFLOWER COMPACT

This day, before we came to harbour, observing some not well affected to unity and concord, but gave some appearance of faction, it was thought good there should be an association and agreement, that we should combine together in one body, and to submit to such government and governors as we should by common consent agree to make and choose, and set our hands to this that follows, word for word.

IN THE name of God, Amen.

We whose names are underwritten, the loyal subjects of our dread sovereign Lord, King James, by the grace of God, of Great Britain, France and Ireland king, defender of the faith, etc., having undertaken, for the glory of God, and advancement of the Christian faith, and honor of our king and country, a voyage to plant the first colony in the Northern parts of Virginia, do by these presents solemnly and mutually in the presence of God, and one of another, covenant and combine ourselves together into a civil body politic, for our better ordering and preservation and furtherance of the ends aforesaid; and by virtue hereof to enact, constitute, and frame such just and equal laws, ordinances, acts, constitutions, and offices, from time to time, as shall be thought most meet and convenient for the general good of the colony, unto which we promise all due submission and obedience.

In witness whereof we have hereunder subscribed our names at Cape-Cod the 11 of November, in the year of the reign of our sovereign lord, King James, of England, France, and Ireland the eighteenth, and of Scotland the fifty-fourth. Anno Domini 1620.[1]

DAY 1
FOR THE GLORY OF GOD

SCRIPTURE READING

Jesus said these things, then lifting up his eyes to heaven, he said, "Father, the time has come. <u>Glorify</u> your Son, that your Son may also <u>glorify</u> you; even as you gave him authority over all flesh, so he will give eternal life to all whom you have given him. This is eternal life, that they should know you, the only true God, and him whom you sent, Jesus Christ. I <u>glorified</u> you on the earth. I have accomplished the work which you have given me to do. Now, Father, <u>glorify</u> me with your own self with the <u>glory</u> which I had with you before the world existed.

"I revealed your name to the people whom you have given me out of the world. They were yours, and you have given them to me. They have kept your word. Now they have known that all things whatever you have given me are from you, for the words which you have given me I have given to them; and they received them, and knew for sure that I came from you. They have believed that you sent me. I pray for them. I don't pray for the world, but for those whom you have given me, for they are yours. All things that are mine are yours, and yours are mine, and I am <u>glorified</u> in them. I am no more in the world, but these are in the world, and I am coming to you. Holy Father, keep them through your name which you have given me, that they may be one, even as we are. While I was with them in the world, I kept them in your name. I have kept those whom you have given me. None of them is lost except the son of destruction, that the Scripture might be fulfilled. But now I come to you, and I say these things in the world, that they may have my joy made full in themselves. I have given them your word. The world hated them because they are not of the world, even as I am not of the world. I pray not that you would take them from the world, but that you would keep them from the evil one. They are not of the world, even as I am not of the world. Sanctify them in your truth. Your word is truth. As you sent me into the world, even <u>so I have sent them into the world</u>. For their sakes I sanctify myself, that they themselves also may be sanctified in truth.

"Not for these only do I pray, but for those also who will believe in me through their word, that they may all be one; even as you, Father, are in me, and I in you, that they also may be one in us; that the world may believe that you sent me. The <u>glory</u> which you have given me, I have given to them, that they may be one, even as we are one, I in them, and you in me, that they may be perfected into one, that the world may know that you sent me and loved them, even as you loved me. Father, I desire that they also whom you have given me be with me where I am, that they may see my <u>glory</u> which you have given me, for you loved me before the foundation of the world. Righteous Father, the world hasn't known you, but I knew you; and these knew that you sent me. I made known to them your name, and will make it known; that the love with which you loved me may be in them, and I in them." (John 17:1-26)

EXPLANATION

Glorifying God is a theme in this chapter in the book of John. Jesus spoke all the words you just read. I counted eight times that he used the word glory or glorify. It means to honor, praise, and worship. It also means to magnify and make renowned.

Jesus glorified God because he accomplished the work that God gave him to do. So, what did he do exactly? He revealed God's name to the people God gave him, he taught them God's word, and he kept everyone God gave him. He's talking about believers, people who have put their faith in Jesus. That's who God gave to Jesus. And Jesus didn't lose any true believers to the enemy, Satan.

While Jesus was talking to God about how he glorified him, he prayed for all the believers. If you've put your faith in him, that prayer is meant for you. He revealed that he's given his very own glory to believers. What's more is that Jesus is in turn glorified in believers. That's right, you bring him glory.

Now just as Jesus was sent into the world to bring God glory, he sends each of us into the world to do likewise. The work he's given us to do includes sharing God's word with others so they can be saved (Matthew 28:18-20), bearing much fruit (John 15:8), and being a light among the darkness (Matthew 5:14-16).

Jesus ended his prayer by stating that we'll see him in heaven one day and get to witness his full glory firsthand.

LESSON

The Mayflower was a ship that brought the very first Pilgrims from England to America in 1620 where they founded Plymouth Colony in present day Massachusetts. The passengers created the Mayflower Compact.

The Mayflower Compact states the reason the people embarked on their journey to America. "...having undertaken, for the glory of God, and advancement of the Christian faith, ... in the presence of God, ... covenant and combine ourselves together into a civil body politic." They did it to bring God glory and fulfill Jesus's commission to spread the gospel!

In the presence of God, they joined together in their mission. That's exactly what Jesus asks each of us to do. But before we can join together with others, we must be plugged into Jesus. The way Jesus describes how glory works between believers and him makes me think of an everlasting battery. Jesus is the glory source we believers must plug into. You, Christian, are a Jesus charged, everlasting battery of glory. The more you're plugged into Jesus, the more glory charge you're going to get, be able to radiate, and reflect back to Jesus.

Think of how much God has blessed the United States since its creation. It's because our founders were plugged into the source of glory, Jesus, and united in their mission to bring him glory. We share the same mission as our nation's founders. Plug into Jesus today.

Are you plugged into the source of glory so that you can glorify God? If you haven't put your faith in Jesus Christ, that's the first step. That's how you connect to the source of glory.

Next, you've got to stay connected to the source. Your cell phone loses power as you use it throughout the day and you eventually have to charge the battery if you want to keep using it. It's the same with you. Life and all the difficulties it throws at you are going to drain away your ability to fulfill your mission to spread God's word. Stay connected to Jesus every day through prayer, reading your Bible, listening to worship music, and fellowshipping with other Christians.

APPLICATION

Today, think of yourself as a glory battery. Connect to Jesus by trusting him with your life, your salvation, and your mission in life. Identify anything in your life that drains your battery and replace it with something that'll recharge it instead. Do you have time to read a romance or thriller novel each day but don't have time to read the Bible? Plug into Jesus instead of the world and let his glory power your life.

PRAYER

Dear God, thank you for sending Jesus to give us the example of how to glorify you. I want to plug into Jesus, the source of all glory, today and every day going forward. I know that I'm a sinner and that Jesus died for me. I believe that Jesus rose from the dead and is in heaven where I'll see his full glory one day. Please help me stop draining my glory battery by plugging into worldly and sinful things. Instead, help me turn from my sin, focus on righteous living, reading the Bible, and praying so that I can be filled with Jesus's glory and fulfill the same mission our nation's founders had, spreading the gospel through my words and deeds. I want to live for the glory of God.

THE DECLARATION OF INDEPENDENCE

In Congress, July 4, 1776.

The unanimous Declaration of the thirteen united States of America, When in the Course of human events, it becomes necessary for one people to dissolve the political bands which have connected them with another, and to assume among the powers of the earth, the separate and <u>equal station to which the Laws of Nature and of Nature's God entitle them</u>, a decent respect to the opinions of mankind requires that they should declare the causes which impel them to the separation.

We hold these truths to be self-evident, that <u>all men are created equal</u>, that they are <u>endowed by their Creator with certain unalienable Rights</u>, that among these are <u>Life</u>, <u>Liberty</u> and <u>the pursuit of Happiness</u>.--That to secure these rights, Governments are instituted among Men, deriving their just powers from the consent of the governed, --That whenever any Form of Government becomes destructive of these ends, it is the Right of the People to alter or to abolish it, and to institute new Government, laying its foundation on such principles and organizing its powers in such form, as to them shall seem most likely to effect their Safety and Happiness. Prudence, indeed, will dictate that Governments long established should not be changed for light and transient causes; and accordingly all experience hath shewn, that mankind are more disposed to suffer, while evils are sufferable, than to right themselves by abolishing the forms to which they are accustomed. But when a long train of abuses and usurpations, pursuing invariably the same Object evinces a design to reduce them under absolute Despotism, it is their right, it is their duty, to throw off such Government, and to provide new Guards for their future security.--Such has been the patient sufferance of these Colonies; and such is now the necessity which constrains them to alter their former Systems of Government. The history of the present King of Great Britain is a history of repeated injuries and usurpations, all having in direct object the establishment of an absolute Tyranny over these States. To prove this, let Facts be submitted to a candid world.

He has refused his Assent to Laws, the most wholesome and necessary for the public good.

He has forbidden his Governors to pass Laws of immediate and pressing importance, unless suspended in their operation till his Assent should be obtained; and when so suspended, he has utterly neglected to attend to them.

He has refused to pass other Laws for the accommodation of large districts of people, unless those people would relinquish the right of Representation in the Legislature, a right inestimable to them and formidable to tyrants only.

He has called together legislative bodies at places unusual, uncomfortable, and distant from the depository of their public Records, for the sole purpose of fatiguing them into compliance with his measures.

He has dissolved Representative Houses repeatedly, for opposing with manly firmness his invasions on the rights of the people.

He has refused for a long time, after such dissolutions, to cause others to be elected; whereby the Legislative powers, incapable of Annihilation, have returned to the People at large for their exercise; the State remaining in the mean time exposed to all the dangers of invasion from without, and convulsions within.

He has endeavoured to prevent the population of these States; for that purpose obstructing the Laws for Naturalization of Foreigners; refusing to pass others to encourage their migrations hither, and raising the conditions of new Appropriations of Lands.

He has obstructed the Administration of Justice, by refusing his Assent to Laws for establishing Judiciary powers.

He has made Judges dependent on his Will alone, for the tenure of their offices, and the amount and payment of their salaries.

He has erected a multitude of New Offices, and sent hither swarms of Officers to harrass our people, and eat out their substance.

He has kept among us, in times of peace, Standing Armies without the Consent of our legislatures.

He has affected to render the Military independent of and superior to the Civil power.

He has combined with others to subject us to a jurisdiction foreign to our constitution, and unacknowledged by our laws; giving his Assent to their Acts of pretended Legislation:

For Quartering large bodies of armed troops among us:

For protecting them, by a mock Trial, from punishment for any Murders which they should commit on the Inhabitants of these States:

For cutting off our Trade with all parts of the world:

For imposing Taxes on us without our Consent:

For depriving us in many cases, of the benefits of Trial by Jury:

For transporting us beyond Seas to be tried for pretended offences

For abolishing the free System of English Laws in a neighbouring Province, establishing therein an Arbitrary government, and enlarging its Boundaries so as to render it at once an example and fit instrument for introducing the same absolute rule into these Colonies:

For taking away our Charters, abolishing our most valuable Laws, and altering fundamentally the Forms of our Governments:

For suspending our own Legislatures, and declaring themselves invested with power to legislate for us in all cases whatsoever.

He has abdicated Government here, by declaring us out of his Protection and waging War against us.

He has plundered our seas, ravaged our Coasts, burnt our towns, and destroyed the lives of our people.

He is at this time transporting large Armies of foreign Mercenaries to compleat the works of death, desolation and tyranny, already begun with circumstances of Cruelty & perfidy scarcely paralleled in the most barbarous ages, and totally unworthy the Head of a civilized nation.

He has constrained our fellow Citizens taken Captive on the high Seas to bear Arms against their Country, to become the executioners of their friends and Brethren, or to fall themselves by their Hands.

He has excited domestic insurrections amongst us, and has endeavoured to bring on the inhabitants of our frontiers, the merciless Indian Savages, whose known rule of warfare, is an undistinguished destruction of all ages, sexes and conditions.

In every stage of these Oppressions We have Petitioned for Redress in the most humble terms: Our repeated Petitions have been answered only by repeated injury. A Prince whose character is thus marked by every act which may define a Tyrant, is unfit to be the ruler of a free people.

Nor have We been wanting in attentions to our Brittish brethren. We have warned them from time to time of attempts by their legislature to extend an unwarrantable jurisdiction over us. We have reminded them of the circumstances of our emigration and settlement here. We have appealed to their native justice and magnanimity, and we have conjured them by the ties of our common kindred to disavow these usurpations, which, would inevitably interrupt our connections and correspondence. They too have been deaf to the voice of justice and of consanguinity. We must, therefore, acquiesce in the necessity, which denounces our Separation, and hold them, as we hold the rest of mankind, Enemies in War, in Peace Friends.

We, therefore, the Representatives of the united States of America, in General Congress, Assembled, <u>appealing to the Supreme Judge of the world for the rectitude of our intentions</u>, do, in the Name, and by Authority of the good People of these Colonies, solemnly publish and declare, That these United Colonies are, and of Right ought to be Free and Independent States; that they are Absolved from all Allegiance to the British Crown, and that all political connection between them and the State of Great Britain, is and ought to be totally dissolved; and that as Free and Independent States, they have full Power to levy War, conclude Peace, contract Alliances, establish Commerce, and to do all other Acts and Things which Independent States may of right do. And for the support of this Declaration, with a firm reliance on the protection of divine Providence, we mutually pledge to each other our Lives, our Fortunes and our sacred Honor.[2]

DAY 2
CREATED EQUAL

SCRIPTURE READING

God created man in his own image. In God's image he created him; male and female he created them. (Genesis 1:27)

For the wrath of God is revealed from heaven against all ungodliness and unrighteousness of men who suppress the truth in unrighteousness, because that which is known of God is revealed in them, for God revealed it to them. For the invisible things of him since the creation of the world are clearly seen, being perceived through the things that are made, even his everlasting power and divinity, that they may be without excuse. Because knowing God, they didn't glorify him as God, and didn't give thanks, but became vain in their reasoning, and their senseless heart was darkened. (Romans 1:18-21)

If you will confess with your mouth that Jesus is Lord and believe in your heart that God raised him from the dead, you will be saved. For with the heart one believes resulting in righteousness; and with the mouth confession is made resulting in salvation. For the Scripture says, "Whoever believes in him will not be disappointed."

For there is no distinction between Jew and Greek; for the same Lord is Lord of all, and is rich to all who call on him. For, "Whoever will call on the name of the Lord will be saved." (Romans 10:9-13)

For as many as are led by the Spirit of God, these are children of God. For you didn't receive the spirit of bondage again to fear, but you received the Spirit of adoption, by whom we cry, "Abba! Father!"

For by grace you have been saved through faith, and that not of yourselves; it is the gift of God, not of works, that no one would boast. (Ephesians 2:8-9)

The Spirit himself testifies with our spirit that we are children of God; and if children, then heirs—heirs of God and joint heirs with Christ, if indeed we suffer with him, that we may also be glorified with him. (Romans 8:14-17)

EXPLANATION

Here we learn that God created every single person in his own image. Men and women have God's image in common. We're all equal in this way.

God makes it clear that even though we can't see him while we dwell here on earth his presence is unmistakable. He reveals himself to us through everything he's made. No one will have an excuse for being an atheist or agnostic when they meet Jesus face to face. This is something else we all have in common. God has revealed himself to everyone.

Yet God also revealed himself physically thousands of years ago when he came down from heaven and took on the form of man. That's Jesus, God in the flesh. Jesus died to save every single person who has ever lived. Jesus is a Jew, but there's no distinction between Jew or Greek when it comes to salvation. Now Greek is a term which refers to anyone who isn't Jewish, so that's likely most of you reading this. It doesn't matter what your nationality or background is. Jesus died to save everyone. We're equal in this manner too.

What's more is that it doesn't matter what you've done to try to earn your salvation. It doesn't matter. It's not about what you've done. It's about what Jesus did. Salvation isn't earned, it's a gift.

The last thing we learn in the Scripture reading today is that everyone who believes, who has put their saving faith in Jesus, becomes a child of God. Every believer is an heir of God and a joint heir with Jesus.

We were all created equal, saved equal, and we believers all inherit eternal life equal.

LESSON

The Declaration of Independence was written by our nation's founding fathers in 1776. Here's what they said regarding equality: "When...it becomes necessary...for people to...assume...equal station to which...Nature's God entitle them.... We hold these truths to be self-evident, that all men are created equal." They recognized the truth the Scriptures you read today revealed, that we're all created equal in

God's eyes and we each have the God given right to be treated as such.

APPLICATION

Every single person is made in the image of God. Do you ignore the elderly, needy, or homeless? Do you look down upon people with less education than you, who have a different color of skin than you, who are trapped in a life of sin, or who vote different than you? Today, know that God created them just like he created you. God loves them the same as he loves you. Jesus died to save them when he died to save you too. Pray for someone you haven't treated with the respect they deserve and ask God to give you a heart full of compassion for everyone.

Do you truly believe what God has said, that we're all saved equal? If you're trying to earn your way into heaven, your effort is futile. You can't outdo what Jesus already did for you. Today, know and believe that it doesn't matter how much sin is in your past or how much good you've done since being saved. You are saved by the blood of Jesus regardless. Pray for God's forgiveness and be at peace.

PRAYER

Dear God, thank you for creating all of us equal in your image, for revealing yourself to us through your creation, and for sending Jesus to die for every one of us no matter our degree of sin. I can't wait to enter heaven and see the original design in which I was created from. Please forgive me for how I've treated others in the past. Help me love all people the way that you love us. Please forgive me for trying to earn my way into heaven when I know that believing in Jesus is the only way into heaven. Help me be at peace knowing that I'm saved and that nothing can take that away.

DAY 3
ENDOWED WITH LIFE

SCRIPTURE READING

Jesus therefore said to them, "Most certainly, I tell you, it wasn't Moses who gave you the bread out of heaven, but my Father gives you the true bread out of heaven. For the bread of God is that which comes down out of heaven and gives life to the world."

They said therefore to him, "Lord, always give us this bread."

Jesus said to them, "I am the bread of life. Whoever comes to me will not be hungry, and whoever believes in me will never be thirsty." (John 6:32-35)

Jesus answered her, "If you knew the gift of God, and who it is who says to you, 'Give me a drink,' you would have asked him, and he would have given you living water."

The woman said to him, "Sir, you have nothing to draw with, and the well is deep. So where do you get that living water? Are you greater than our father Jacob, who gave us the well and drank from it himself, as did his children and his livestock?"

Jesus answered her, "Everyone who drinks of this water will thirst again, but whoever drinks of the water that I will give him will never thirst again; but the water that I will give him will become in him a well of water springing up to eternal life." (John 4:10-14)

Jesus therefore said to them again, "...The thief only comes to steal, kill, and destroy. I came that they may have life, and may have it abundantly." (John 10:7, 10)

Again, therefore, Jesus spoke to them, saying, "I am the light of the world. He who follows me will not walk in the darkness, but will have the light of life." (John 8:12)

EXPLANATION

In the Scripture reading for today, we see several ways in which Jesus gives us life.

Jesus is the bread of life. Bread provides nourishment to your body. It enables you to function and to grow. It's the same with Jesus. The Bible describes him as the Word of God. We're to feast upon his Word and desire his pure truth so that we can be saved and then grow in our faith. By believing in Jesus, we're promised eternal life. That's a life in which we'll never be hungry or thirsty.

Jesus is also living water. He described it like a well springing up. His water is never ending. When you put your faith in Jesus, his Holy Spirit fills you up and seals you with Jesus's guarantee of eternal life. What's more is that the Holy Spirit is always with you, teaching you all things, and guiding your life.

If you're partaking of the bread of life and the living water, then out of your own life will flow Jesus's light. You'll have the abundant life that Jesus spoke of. A life that reflects his light in a world that's full of darkness and doesn't know him.

LESSON

In the Declaration of Independence, the founding fathers noted three truths. "We hold these truths to be self-evident, ... that they are endowed by their Creator with certain unalienable Rights, that among these are Life." An unalienable right is something that can't be surrendered or taken away. America's founders knew that God endowed or gave people certain rights. Life is one of those rights.

Yesterday, you learned that God created you specifically in his image. He certainly wants you to live. If he didn't, he simply just wouldn't have created you to begin with. Yet he did. There's a reason for that.

What's most important is that God wants you to have eternal life. He's not content with you living for a mere earthly existence. God is eternal and he created you with eternity in mind. You are meant to live with him in eternity.

You certainly have a right to life, but more importantly to eternal life. As the bread of life, the living water, and the light of the world, Jesus is the only way to that eternal life.

APPLICATION

Consider how you are living your life. Are you living for earth or for heaven? If you're striving to achieve earthly wealth or recognition at the expense of more important eternal things, then you're not living the abundant life that Jesus calls you to. Life on earth is temporary. We can't take anything with us into eternity, and we're living in the last days before Jesus returns.

Today, live your life in recognition of its brevity and be a citizen of heaven. Here are some suggestions. Pray for someone other than yourself. Spend time talking with someone you've neglected. Give anonymously to a charitable cause that fosters life. Share the gospel with someone who doesn't know Jesus. Consume the bread of life by reading your Bible.

PRAYER

Dear God, thank you for giving me life and not just an earthly life, but also a path to eternal life. Thank you for sending Jesus to be my bread of life. Shine your light on anything in my life that I've forsaken in my quest to live a worldly life. Please help me live an abundant life that's focused on heaven and not earth. Help me spend time with you, reading your Word, and praying so that I can be filled with your living water.

DAY 4
ENDOWED WITH LIBERTY

SCRIPTURE READING

Jesus therefore said to those Jews who had believed him, "If you remain in my word, then you are truly my disciples. You will know the truth, and the truth will make you free."

They answered him, "We are Abraham's offspring, and have never been in bondage to anyone. How do you say, 'You will be made free'?"

Jesus answered them, "Most certainly I tell you, everyone who commits sin is the bondservant of sin. A bondservant doesn't live in the house forever. A son remains forever. If therefore the Son makes you free, you will be free indeed." (John 8:31-36)

But thanks be to God that, whereas you were bondservants of sin, you became obedient from the heart to that form of teaching to which you were delivered. Being made free from sin, you became bondservants of righteousness.

I speak in human terms because of the weakness of your flesh; for as you presented your members as servants to uncleanness and to wickedness upon wickedness, even so now present your members as servants to righteousness for sanctification. For when you were servants of sin, you were free from righteousness. What fruit then did you have at that time in the things of which you are now ashamed? For the end of those things is death. But now, being made free from sin and having become servants of God, you have your fruit of sanctification and the result of eternal life. For the wages of sin is death, but the free gift of God is eternal life in Christ Jesus our Lord. (Romans 6:17-23)

Now the Lord is the Spirit; and where the Spirit of the Lord is, there is liberty. (2 Corinthians 3:17)

EXPLANATION

The "truth will make you free." God's word is the truth. So, what does it free you from? The bondage of sin.

Sin is anything that's contrary to God. We're all born sinners. No one is a good person. Even our thoughts condemn us. God's judgment against sin and disobedience is death. This isn't earthly death. This is eternal death and separation from God. That's because God is perfect and holy, so sin can't dwell in heaven.

The opposite of death is life. God gives everyone who believes in Jesus eternal life. He's the pathway to freedom from sin and death. Jesus rescued you from eternal death by dying for your sins. If you've placed your faith in him then you have been set free.

It doesn't end there though. It also means you are no longer a slave, here on earth, to your sinful nature. Sin no longer controls you. The Holy Spirit lives inside of you and guides your life now.

If you let Jesus lead you, if you obey his Word, then you'll live in liberty and righteousness and become a willing servant of God.

LESSON

In the Declaration of Independence, the founding fathers noted three truths. "We hold these truths to be self-evident, ... that they are endowed by their Creator with certain unalienable Rights, that among these are ... Liberty." Liberty or freedom is the second right that the founders knew was God given.

With God's spirit dwelling in the heart of our nation's founders, is it any wonder that we live in the land of the free? "Where the Spirit of the Lord is, there is liberty."

It doesn't matter what you've done in your past. Jesus can forgive it. He can set you free. If Jesus is dwelling in your heart, then you are eternally free. Free from eternal death and a life enslaved by sin. You have the hope and confidence of eternal life. Jesus's Holy Spirit will now help you lead a life reflecting your freedom from sin.

APPLICATION

If you live in America, then you're living in the land of free. But have you personally been set free from all the sin that's got you chained? Putting your faith in Jesus is just the beginning. You're in a daily war with your sinful nature. Today, give Jesus a sin that continues to trip you up and weigh you down.

PRAYER

Dear God, thank you for granting me true liberty through Jesus and for breaking the chains of my sin. Please forgive me for being a sinner. I struggle daily to overcome my sinful nature. I give you this sin that I continue to struggle with. I don't want to be chained down by it any longer. Help me be free of it. Keep me from the temptation of it. Instead, fill me with your Holy Spirit and give me a desire to live a life that reflects my true freedom from sin.

DAY 5
ENDOWED WITH THE PURSUIT OF HAPPINESS

SCRIPTURE READING

What do people really get for all their hard work? I have seen the burden God has placed on us all. Yet God has made everything beautiful for its own time. He has planted eternity in the human heart, but even so, people cannot see the whole scope of God's work from beginning to end. So I concluded there is nothing better than to be happy and enjoy ourselves as long as we can. And people should eat and drink and enjoy the fruits of their labor, for these are gifts from God. (Ecclesiastes 3:9-13 NLT)

Finally, my brothers, rejoice in the Lord! To write the same things to you, to me indeed is not tiresome, but for you it is safe. ...

Not that I have already obtained, or am already made perfect; but I press on, that I may take hold of that for which also I was taken hold of by Christ Jesus.

Brothers, I don't regard myself as yet having taken hold, but one thing I do: forgetting the things which are behind and stretching forward to the things which are before, I press on toward the goal for the prize of the high calling of God in Christ Jesus. (Philippians 3:1, 12-14)

Rejoice in the Lord always! Again I will say, "Rejoice!" Let your gentleness be known to all men. The Lord is at hand. In nothing be anxious, but in everything, by prayer and petition with thanksgiving, let your requests be made known to God. And the peace of God, which surpasses all understanding, will guard your hearts and your thoughts in Christ Jesus.

Finally, brothers, whatever things are true, whatever things are honorable, whatever things are just, whatever things are pure, whatever things are lovely, whatever things are of good report: if there is any virtue and if there is anything worthy of praise, think about these things. Do the things which you learned, received, heard, and saw in me, and the God of peace will be with you. (Philippians 4:4-9)

EXPLANATION

King Solomon pondered the point of life and the benefit of hard work. He knew that God made us for eternity and that life here on earth is just temporary. He realized that since we have nothing to worry about regarding our eternal future, that we can be happy and enjoy the fruits of our labor here on earth. Life and everything in it are gifts from God.

The apostle Paul further explains to us that we are to rejoice. It's commanded. He even told us the reason for that. It's because it is "safe." That means it protects or safeguards your faith. That's an important truth to remember. When you let your emotions weigh you down, doubt enters and that can easily turn into fear, anger, and a whole host of other negative feelings.

Paul then tells us how to be happy. He tells us to stop being anxious. That means stop worrying, being troubled, and fearful. We're to forget about the past, look forward to the future, keep moving forward, pray to God, give thanks to God, and then receive God's peace. Then we're to keep our thoughts focused on honest, pure, and praiseworthy things.

You see, Paul knew the key to happiness is the opposite of anxiety. It's peace and contentment. It's God's peace that's required to guard our hearts and thoughts from what eats away at our happiness.

LESSON

The last self-evident truth that the founding fathers noted in the Declaration of Independence is happiness. "We hold these truths to be self-evident, ... that they are endowed by their Creator with certain unalienable Rights, that among these are ... the pursuit of Happiness."

I want you to note that the founders didn't say "achieve the American dream." You know, get married, buy a house, have kids, get an education, a great paying job, etc. Yet, that's what the world wants us to believe is the pathway to happiness. In a quest to constantly achieve in order to be happy, nothing will ever be enough. So, then you'll never be happy. The reality of it is that's the road that leads to anxiety.

The founding fathers did recognize that happiness is a pursuit. You must follow God and love him with all your heart. Because true happiness is found in the peace that God provides. It's not dependent on earthly circumstance because that's just temporary. It's a confidence in your eternal future that brings joy.

APPLICATION

Today, consider how you are pursuing happiness. Have you been going at it as the world does, by striving to achieve? Make a list of the things you think you have to achieve in your life, or that you must accomplish for God, or that your children must excel at, or ... in order for you to be happy. Now, release all of that to God. Give him your worries about not attaining those things. Ask him for his peace in return.

PRAYER

Dear God, the pursuit of happiness is most certainly a daily struggle. Thank you for showing me the path to true happiness. Please forgive me for trying to achieve joy and happiness in my life the way the world pursues it. Take my list of things I thought I had to accomplish in order to be happy. You can also have the anxiety I've been holding on to regarding how to achieve these things. Please give me your peace and contentment in return. Help me come to you from now on for the peace that happiness requires.

WASHINGTON'S INAUGURAL ADDRESS

April 30, 1789
Fellow Citizens of the Senate and the House of Representatives.

Among the vicissitudes incident to life, no event could have filled me with greater anxieties than that of which the notification was transmitted by your order, and received on the fourteenth day of the present month. On the one hand, I was summoned by my Country, whose voice I can never hear but with veneration and love, from a retreat which I had chosen with the fondest predilection, and, in my flattering hopes, with an immutable decision, as the asylum of my declining years: a retreat which was rendered every day more necessary as well as more dear to me, by the addition of habit to inclination, and of frequent interruptions in my health to the gradual waste committed on it by time. On the other hand, the magnitude and difficulty of the trust to which the voice of my Country called me, being sufficient to awaken in the wisest and most experienced of her citizens, a distrustful scrutiny into his qualifications, could not but overwhelm with dispondence, one, who, inheriting inferior endowments from nature and unpractised in the duties of civil administration, ought to be peculiarly conscious of his own deficiencies. In this conflict of emotions, all I dare aver, is, that it has been my faithful study to collect my duty from a just appreciation of every circumstance, by which it might be affected. All I dare hope, is, that, if in executing this task I have been too much swayed by a grateful remembrance of former instances, or by an affectionate sensibility to this transcendent proof, of the confidence of my fellow-citizens; and have thence too little consulted my incapacity as well as disinclination for the weighty and untried cares before me; my error will be palliated by the motives which misled me, and its consequences be judged by my Country, with some share of the partiality in which they originated.

Such being the impressions under which I have, in obedience to the public summons, repaired to the present station; it would be peculiarly improper to omit in this first official Act, <u>my fervent supplications to that Almighty Being who rules over the Universe</u>, who presides in the Councils of Nations, and whose providential aids can supply every human defect, that his benediction may consecrate to the liberties and happiness of the People of the United States, a Government instituted by themselves for these essential purposes: and may enable every instrument employed in its administration to execute with success, the functions allotted to his charge. <u>In tendering this homage to the Great Author of every public and private good</u> I assure myself that it expresses your sentiments not less than my own; nor those of my fellow-citizens at large, less than either. <u>No People can be bound to acknowledge and adore the invisible hand, which conducts the Affairs of men more than the People of the United States</u>. Every step, by which they have advanced to the character of an independent nation, seems to have been distinguished by some token of providential agency. And in the important revolution just accomplished in the system of their United Government, the tranquil deliberations and voluntary consent of so many distinct communities, from which the event has resulted, cannot be compared with the means by which most Governments have been established, <u>without some return of pious gratitude along with an humble anticipation of the future blessings which the past seem to presage</u>. These reflections, arising out of the present crisis, have forced themselves too strongly on my mind to be suppressed. You will join with me I trust in thinking, that there are none under the influence of which, the proceedings of a new and free Government can more auspiciously commence.

By the article establishing the Executive Department, it is made the duty of the President "to recommend to your consideration, such measures as he shall judge necessary and expedient." The circumstances under which I now meet you, will acquit me from entering into that subject, farther than to refer to the Great Constitutional Charter under which you are assembled; and which, in defining your powers, designates the objects to which your attention is to be given. It will be more consistent with those circumstances, and far more congenial with the feelings which actuate me, to substitute, in place of a recommendation of particular measures, the tribute that is due to the talents, the rectitude, and the patriotism which adorn the characters selected to devise and adopt them. In these honorable qualifications, I behold the surest pledges, that as on one side, no local prejudices, or attachments; no seperate views, nor party animosities, will misdirect the comprehensive and equal eye which ought to watch over this great assemblage of communities and interests: so, on another, that the foundations of our National policy will be laid in the pure and immutable principles of private morality; and the pre-eminence of a free Government, be exemplified by all the attributes which can win the affections of its Citizens, and command the respect of the world.

I dwell on this prospect with every satisfaction which an ardent love for my Country can inspire: <u>since there is no truth more thoroughly established, than that there exists in the economy and course of nature, an indissoluble union between virtue and happiness</u>, between duty and advantage, between the genuine maxims of an honest and magnanimous policy, and the solid rewards of public prosperity and felicity: <u>Since we ought to be no less persuaded that the propitious smiles of Heaven, can never be expected on a nation that disregards the eternal rules of order and right, which Heaven itself has ordained</u>: And since the preservation of the sacred fire of liberty, and the destiny of the Republican model of Government, are justly considered as deeply, perhaps as finally staked, on the experiment entrusted to the hands of the American people.

Besides the ordinary objects submitted to your care, it will remain with your judgment to decide, how far an exercise of the occasional power delegated by the Fifth article of the Constitution is rendered expedient at the present juncture by the nature of objections which have been urged against the System, or by the degree of inquietude which has given birth to them. Instead of undertaking particular recommendations on this subject, in which I could be guided by no lights derived from official opportunities, I shall again give way to my entire confidence in your discernment and pursuit of the public good: For I assure myself that whilst you carefully avoid every alteration which might endanger the benefits of an United and effective Government, or which ought to await the future lessons of experience; a reverence for the characteristic rights of freemen, and a regard for the public harmony, will sufficiently influence your deliberations on the question how far the former can be more impregnably fortified, or the latter be safely and advantageously promoted.

To the preceeding observations I have one to add, which will be most properly addressed to the House of Representatives. It concerns myself, and will therefore be as brief as possible. When I was first honoured with a call into the Service of my Country, then on the eve of an arduous struggle for its liberties, the light in which I contemplated my duty required that I should renounce every pecuniary compensation. From this resolution I have in no instance departed. And being still under the impressions which produced it, I must decline as inapplicable to myself, any share in the personal emoluments, which may be indispensably included in a permanent provision for the Executive Department; and must accordingly pray that the pecuniary estimates for the Station in which I am placed, may, during my continuance in it, be limited to such actual expenditures as the public good may be thought to require.

Having thus imparted to you my sentiments, as they have been awakened by the occasion which brings us together, I shall take my present leave; but not without <u>resorting once more to the benign parent of the human race, in humble supplication that since he has been pleased to favour the American people</u>, with opportunities for deliberating in perfect tranquility, and dispositions for deciding with unparellelled unanimity on a form of Government, for the security of their Union, and the advancement of their happiness; so <u>his divine blessing may be equally conspicuous in the enlarged views, the temperate consultations, and the wise measures on which the success of this Government must depend</u>.[3]

DAY 6
SUPPLICATIONS TO THE ALMIGHTY

SCRIPTURE READING

This is the boldness which we have toward him, that if we ask anything according to his will, he listens to us. And if we know that he listens to us, whatever we ask, we know that we have the petitions which we have asked of him. (1 John 5:14-15)

As they passed by in the morning, they saw the fig tree withered away from the roots. Peter, remembering, said to him, "Rabbi, look! The fig tree which you cursed has withered away."

Jesus answered them, "Have faith in God. For most certainly I tell you, whoever may tell this mountain, 'Be taken up and cast into the sea,' and doesn't doubt in his heart, but believes that what he says is happening, he shall have whatever he says. Therefore I tell you, all things whatever you pray and ask for, believe that you have received them, and you shall have them." (Mark 11:20-24)

Put on the whole armor of God, that you may be able to stand against the wiles of the devil. For our wrestling is not against flesh and blood, but against the principalities, against the powers, against the world's rulers of the darkness of this age, and against the spiritual forces of wickedness in the heavenly places. Therefore put on the whole armor of God, that you may be able to withstand in the evil day, and having done all, to stand. Stand therefore, having the utility belt of truth buckled around your waist, and having put on the breastplate of righteousness, and having fitted your feet with the preparation of the Good News of peace, above all, taking up the shield of faith, with which you will be able to quench all the fiery darts of the evil one. And take the helmet of salvation, and the sword of the Spirit, which is the word of God; with all prayer and requests, praying at all times in the Spirit, and being watchful to this end in all perseverance and requests for all the saints. (Ephesians 6:11-18)

EXPLANATION

Prayer is the theme of today's Bible reading. We're told that we can ask God for anything and it'll be done. However, there's a big caveat. The request must be in accordance with God's will. That means God isn't a genie intent on granting our wishes.

What does it mean to be in God's will? It means you are walking with God, obeying him, and loving him with all your heart. Then you'll be able to pray for things he desires in your life.

Once you've prayed, you must be confident and have faith that God did indeed hear your prayer and that he has every intention of acting upon it. In fact, he always hears the prayers of those who've put their faith in Jesus. Now that doesn't mean we always get what we ask for. God can say no or wait as easily as he says yes.

Remember that Paul the apostle prayed for healing and didn't receive it (2 Corinthians 12:9). God told him his grace was sufficient for him. That Paul's physical weakness allowed God to display his strength all the more through him. Know that if God doesn't say yes to your request that he has a good reason.

You finished today's Scripture reading with the apostle Paul's description of the armor of God. We're living in the very last of the last days before Jesus raptures his believers. Now more than ever, it's important for you to wear this armor and protect yourself from the enemy, Satan. Prayer is a key component of the armor of God and his divine protection. You must pray about everything, at all times, and remember to pray for all believers.

LESSON

President George Washington was the very first president of the United States. He gave his inauguration speech in 1789. Washington recognized the authority of God and the power of prayer. Look at what he said, "…it would be peculiarly improper to omit in this first official Act, my fervent supplications to that Almighty Being who rules over the Universe." Supplications means to ask humbly. The almighty who rules over the universe is none other than God. The very first official act Washington did as president was pray to God!

That makes me smile. Did you see what he prayed for? That God's benediction or blessing would consecrate or be dedicated to the freedom and happiness of the people. And that God would enable the government to fulfill that mission.

We must recognize the power of God and the importance of prayer just as President Washington did. In order for our prayers to God to be effective, we must be filled with Jesus's Holy Spirit so that we're able to walk with God and pray according to his will in our lives. Then we must believe that God heard us and that we'll receive what we asked for.

APPLICATION

Do you pray first thing before embarking on the day or prior to an important task, like President Washington did? Today, choose to make prayer a daily morning habit. If you already pray each morning, then pray throughout the day today. Identify one thing you're going to petition God about today that you believe aligns with his will in your life. Then have faith that God will provide.

PRAYER

Dear God, thank you for hearing my prayers. Please forgive me for not talking with you as often as I should. I pray that you help me make prayer a daily morning habit. Once I've achieved that goal, please help me continue to grow closer to you by making my requests to you throughout the day and before I fall asleep. I believe my petition today aligns with your will in my life. Help me have faith that you heard my request and that I'll receive it.

DAY 7
ADORE THE INVISIBLE HAND

SCRIPTURE READING

Christ is the visible image of the invisible God. He existed before anything was created and is supreme over all creation, for through him God created everything in the heavenly realms and on earth. He made the things we can see and the things we can't see—such as thrones, kingdoms, rulers, and authorities in the unseen world. Everything was created through him and for him. He existed before anything else, and he holds all creation together. Christ is also the head of the church, which is his body. He is the beginning, supreme over all who rise from the dead. So he is first in everything. For God in all his fullness was pleased to live in Christ, and through him God reconciled everything to himself. He made peace with everything in heaven and on earth by means of Christ's blood on the cross. This includes you who were once far away from God. You were his enemies, separated from him by your evil thoughts and actions. Yet now he has reconciled you to himself through the death of Christ in his physical body. As a result, he has brought you into his own presence, and you are holy and blameless as you stand before him without a single fault. (Colossians 1:15-22 NLT)

Jesus said to him, "Because you have seen me, you have believed. Blessed are those who have not seen and have believed." (John 20:29)

Oh come, let's sing to Yahweh. Let's shout aloud to the rock of our salvation! Let's come before his presence with thanksgiving. Let's extol him with songs! For Yahweh is a great God, a great King above all gods. In his hand are the deep places of the earth. The heights of the mountains are also his. The sea is his, and he made it. His hands formed the dry land. Oh come, let's worship and bow down. Let's kneel before Yahweh, our Maker, for he is our God. We are the people of his pasture, and the sheep in his care. Today, oh that you would hear his voice! (Psalm 95:1-7)

EXPLANATION

Today we learn that Jesus is the visible image of the invisible God. He's God in the flesh. As such, he's certainly worthy of our praise because he's supreme over all creation. He created everything we see and even things we can't see. He made the earth just for us.

Jesus is also head of the church. That's a reference to the people who've put their faith in him. Believers are the church. Jesus was also the very first person resurrected from the dead. Since he's risen, we believers can be sure he'll raise us as well!

Jesus died for every single person. He brought peace between you and God. You are now holy and blameless before him. Not only that, but Jesus's crucifixion and resurrection apply to all creation. He redeemed everything that was under God's curse. One day that curse will be lifted and everything and everyone will live in harmony as a result.

As a believer, because you believe what you didn't witness firsthand about Jesus, you are considered blessed. You have much to rejoice about regarding God because of all the wonderful things he's done for you. You are indeed blessed. So, praise him with songs!

LESSON

President George Washington continued his inauguration speech by honoring, adoring, and praising God. "In tendering this homage to the Great Author of every public and private good.... No People can be bound to acknowledge and adore the invisible hand, which conducts the Affairs of men more than the People of the United States." He gave homage, which is high regard, to the Great Author and the invisible hand. That's Jesus. President Washington also knew that we Americans have more to thank and praise God about than other people.

Now think about that for a minute. Washington was the first president of the United States. He didn't see anything compared to what you've seen and read about regarding how great God has been to our nation. America was just beginning when he was president. Look at what it's become today because of God's blessings upon us.

We're meant to recognize Jesus's hand and authority in all creation, redemption, and every blessing. Once we have that recognition, we can't help but adore and worship him for all that he's done for us.

APPLICATION

Do you recognize Jesus's hand in your life? Today, know that Jesus's hand, the visible hand of God, created you. He fashioned Adam from the dust of the earth. He formed you in your mother's womb. He died for you so that you can see him face to face one day and live with him in heaven.

Sing a song either out loud or in your heart to Jesus to show him how much you adore him. Turn to a Christian radio station and sing along. Or think of a Christmas carol about Jesus. "O Come Let Us Adore Him" comes to my mind.

PRAYER

Dear God, you are worthy of my praise and thanksgiving. Thank you for sending Jesus to be your visible image. Thank you for leading me to salvation through Jesus. Thank you for helping me believe in all that Jesus has done for me and all that he has promised me. Thank you for blessing America. Please forgive me for being bitter about what I don't have and envious of what others have. Help me see your hand in my own life and recognize the wonderful things you've specifically done for me.

DAY 8
ANTICIPATE FUTURE BLESSINGS

SCRIPTURE READING

For I consider that the sufferings of this present time are not worthy to be compared with the glory which will be revealed toward us. For the creation waits with eager expectation for the children of God to be revealed. For the creation was subjected to vanity, not of its own will, but because of him who subjected it, in hope that the creation itself also will be delivered from the bondage of decay into the liberty of the glory of the children of God. For we know that the whole creation groans and travails in pain together until now. Not only so, but ourselves also, who have the first fruits of the Spirit, even we ourselves groan within ourselves, waiting for adoption, the redemption of our body. For we were saved in hope, but hope that is seen is not hope. For who hopes for that which he sees? But if we hope for that which we don't see, we wait for it with patience. (Romans 8:18-25)

Now faith is assurance of things hoped for, proof of things not seen. For by this, the elders obtained approval. ...

These all died in faith, not having received the promises, but having seen them and embraced them from afar, and having confessed that they were strangers and pilgrims on the earth. For those who say such things make it clear that they are seeking a country of their own. If indeed they had been thinking of that country from which they went out, they would have had enough time to return. But now they desire a better country, that is, a heavenly one. Therefore God is not ashamed of them, to be called their God, for he has prepared a city for them. (Hebrews 11:1-2, 13-16)

God is not a man, that he should lie, nor a son of man, that he should repent. Has he said, and he won't do it? Or has he spoken, and he won't make it good? (Numbers 23:19)

"You know in all your hearts and in all your souls that not one thing has failed of all the good things which Yahweh your God spoke concerning you. All have happened to you. Not one thing has failed of it." (Joshua 23:14)

Let's hold fast the confession of our hope without wavering; for he who promised is faithful. (Hebrews 10:23)

EXPLANATION

Whatever you are experiencing and suffering through today, it doesn't even compare to the glory, honor, and praise that awaits you in heaven. For everyone and everything in creation is eagerly awaiting the future blessings that God promised.

One such promise is the redemption of our bodies and the earth itself from the curse of sin that brought death and decay. We wait with patient expectation for God's promises like these.

That's what faith is all about. Being confident that you're going to get the very thing that was promised. The elders, the founders of our faith who are spoken of in the Bible, didn't receive all of God's promises while they were alive on earth. They were looking forward to God's promise of heaven.

You can be confident, like our ancestors in the Bible, because God kept his promises in the past regarding Israel and Jesus. Just think of how he delivered the Israelites from Egyptian slavery, gave them manna from heaven each day, and led them into the promised land. Think of how he promised the messiah would come and save people from their sins. Jesus came and did exactly that.

God has fulfilled Bible prophecy. So, you can trust that God will continue to keep all of the promises he's made. He's faithful. His word is truth.

LESSON

In President George Washington's Inaugural speech, he thought back on the revolution and how the government came to be and said, "without some return of pious gratitude along with an humble anticipation of the future blessings which the past seem to presage." Presage means to foretell. Washington recognized that God's faithfulness in the past was an indicator that he'd be faithful in the future as well. Thus, he said we should humbly anticipate future blessings from God.

That's exactly what we learned from the Scriptures today. We should be eagerly and patiently awaiting the fulfillment of God's promises.

Are you confidently anticipating God's future blessings in your own life?

APPLICATION

Today, think of a future promise that God has revealed in the Bible. It could be eternal life, your new immortal body, the end of sin, the new earth, no more sorrow, or Jesus coming in the clouds to rapture the church. Anticipate that promise today. Be confident that God is going to make it happen. It'll grow your faith.

PRAYER

Dear God, thank you for telling us what's going to happen in advance and then making it happen! I know that you are going to make good on all of your promises to me because you always fulfilled your promises in the past. Please forgive me for doubting your plan, for doubting that you're in control, and for doubting that you'll come through. Help me hold on to this one particular future blessing that you've promised for me. Please fill me with your peace so that I can wait patiently and confidently.

DAY 9
VIRTUE AND HAPPINESS

SCRIPTURE READING

Don't fret because of evildoers, neither be envious against those who work unrighteousness. For they shall soon be cut down like the grass, and wither like the green herb. Trust in Yahweh, and do good. Dwell in the land, and enjoy safe pasture. Also delight yourself in Yahweh, and he will give you the desires of your heart. Commit your way to Yahweh. Trust also in him, and he will do this: he will make your righteousness shine out like light, and your justice as the noon day sun. Rest in Yahweh, and wait patiently for him. Don't fret because of him who prospers in his way, because of the man who makes wicked plots happen. ... A man's steps are established by Yahweh. He delights in his way. Though he stumble, he shall not fall, for Yahweh holds him up with his hand. ... Mark the perfect man, and see the upright, for there is a future for the man of peace. (Psalm 37:1-7, 18, 23-24, 37)

Seeing that his divine power has granted to us all things that pertain to life and godliness, through the knowledge of him who called us by his own glory and virtue, by which he has granted to us his precious and exceedingly great promises; that through these you may become partakers of the divine nature, having escaped from the corruption that is in the world by lust. Yes, and for this very cause adding on your part all diligence, in your faith supply moral excellence; and in moral excellence, knowledge; and in knowledge, self-control; and in self-control, perseverance; and in perseverance, godliness; and in godliness, brotherly affection; and in brotherly affection, love. ... For thus you will be richly supplied with the entrance into the eternal Kingdom of our Lord and Savior, Jesus Christ. (2 Peter 1:3-7, 11)

My son, don't forget my teaching, but let your heart keep my commandments, for they will add to you length of days, years of life, and peace. ... Trust in Yahweh with all your heart, and don't lean on your own understanding. In all your ways acknowledge him, and he will make your paths straight. ... Happy is the man who finds wisdom, the man who gets understanding. ... Her ways are ways of pleasantness. All her paths are peace. She is a tree of life to those who lay hold of her. Happy is everyone who retains her. (Proverbs 3:1-2, 5-6, 13, 17-18)

EXPLANATION

In the Scripture reading today, we're instructed not to worry about people who are unrighteous and yet prosper. That's not the way to true happiness.

We're to trust in God and take pleasure in him. If we do, we're promised the desires of our heart in return. That's because we'll desire the same things that God desires for us.

How do you get to the point at which your desire aligns with God's will? Moral excellence is another way to describe virtue. It means conforming to a standard of right and morality. God's standards, his laws, are the ones you must conform to, not the world's, if you want live in his will.

We also learn that we should supplement virtue with knowledge and wisdom. God's Word is the source of truth and wisdom. It leads to peace and happiness. Remember from a previous day that the opposite of happiness is anxiety, so the cure is peace. God's peace will provide you happiness and make you shine like a light. So, we see that virtue and happiness go hand in hand.

Even though you see the wicked prosper here on earth, know that there's a wonderful future ahead for the righteous. There's a grand entrance into the eternal kingdom of Jesus straight ahead for believers like you.

LESSON

President George Washington spoke about virtue and happiness in his Inaugural Address. Here's what he had to say, "since there is no truth more thoroughly established, than that there exists in the economy and course of nature, an indissoluble union between virtue and happiness." He believed the unbreakable link between virtue and happiness that we just learned about is a truth thoroughly established.

He's right. When you place your faith in Jesus, he then fills you with his Holy Spirit who conforms your life to God's standard of virtue. God's standard is the only one that matters. As you grow closer to Jesus, you'll sin less, and you'll become more righteous in your behavior. You're filled with Jesus, so you're becoming more and more like him each day!

Pursuing God's virtuous life instead of the world's standard of morality will fill you with God's peace that will result in your happiness and contentment.

APPLICATION

Consider your beliefs about morality and virtue. Examine if they conform to God's standard. This could be hard for you if you've grown to accept the world's view of morality. It doesn't matter how your friends, your favorite celebrity, your family, or a leader you look up to defines sin. It only matters what God says.

God's Word is clear. Sex outside of God defined marriage between a biological man and a biological woman is a sin. Abortion is a sin. Worshiping the planet and believing man is in control of the environment is a sin.

Today, ask God to help you turn away from the upside-down view of sin that the world promotes. Pray that God gives you a desire to know his Word and live in the light of his truth because it's the only path to happiness.

PRAYER

Dear God, please forgive me for being a sinner and for thinking and acting the way the world wants me to. Help me put on the whole armor of God so that I can protect my faith and deflect the enemy's attacks against your truth. Help me have a desire to read and understand your word and the virtues you teach. Please fill me with your peace so I can experience true happiness.

DAY 10
PROPITIOUS SMILES OF HEAVEN

SCRIPTURE READING

Behold, I have set before you today life and prosperity, and death and evil. For I command you today to love Yahweh your God, to walk in his ways and to keep his commandments, his statutes, and his ordinances, that you may live and multiply, and that Yahweh your God may bless you in the land where you go in to possess it. But if your heart turns away, and you will not hear, but are drawn away and worship other gods, and serve them, I declare to you today that you will surely perish. You will not prolong your days in the land where you pass over the Jordan to go in to possess it. I call heaven and earth to witness against you today that I have set before you life and death, the blessing and the curse. Therefore choose life, that you may live, you and your descendants, to love Yahweh your God, to obey his voice, and to cling to him; for he is your life, and the length of your days. (Deuteronomy 30:15-20)

It shall happen, if you shall listen diligently to Yahweh your God's voice, to observe to do all his commandments which I command you today, that Yahweh your God will set you high above all the nations of the earth. (Deuteronomy 28:1)

Don't you see how wonderfully kind, tolerant, and patient God is with you? Does this mean nothing to you? Can't you see that his kindness is intended to turn you from your sin? But because you are stubborn and refuse to turn from your sin, you are storing up terrible punishment for yourself. For a day of anger is coming, when God's righteous judgment will be revealed. He will judge everyone according to what they have done. He will give eternal life to those who keep on doing good, seeking after the glory and honor and immortality that God offers. But he will pour out his anger and wrath on those who live for themselves, who refuse to obey the truth and instead live lives of wickedness. ... And this is the message I proclaim—that the day is coming when God, through Christ Jesus, will judge everyone's secret life. (Romans 2:4-8, 16 NLT)

EXPLANATION

Today you read about God's promises for blessings and curses, life and death, upon his people. While these promises were spoken over the Israelites as they entered the promised land, they are still applicable and relevant today. Perhaps now more than ever.

It's simple really. If you love God with all your heart, you'll naturally want to obey him. That will then lead to blessings. However, if you don't love God then you're not going to obey him. Instead you'll obey Satan, chase after his false gods, and keep on sinning. This will lead to curses.

If the Israelites obeyed God, he promised to set the nation of Israel high above the nations of the earth. While Israel has certainly been blessed in many ways, this is a promise they haven't received yet. It'll be fulfilled in the future during Jesus's millennial reign on earth.

We further learn that these blessings and curses apply to us individually. The apostle Paul tells us that we'll each be judged according to what we've done here on earth. Even the secret things we've done.

There's a path that leads to eternal blessings and eternal life. Place your faith in Jesus and reap those rewards.

LESSON

President George Washington in his Inaugural Address as our very first national leader forever tied the United States to God's blessings and curses. Here's what he said. "Since we ought to be no less persuaded that the propitious smiles of Heaven, can never be expected on a nation that disregards the eternal rules of order and right, which Heaven itself has ordained." Washington prayed this to God. He recognized that a nation must follow God's rules of right and wrong in order to receive propitious or favorable "smiles of Heaven," which are God's blessings.

You learned above that God promised to lift the nation of Israel high above the other nations if they obeyed him, but it hasn't happened for them yet. It will. Which nation has God lifted up now instead? It's America!

It didn't happen to our nation by accident or because of our own might. It's because our nation was founded with a mission to bring God glory, to advance the gospel, to follow God's rules of order. So, we as a nation have reaped the rewards of being obedient.

However, a nation is comprised of people who must be obedient to God in order for the nation as a whole to be obedient. Choose to love Jesus and follow him with all your heart so that you'll gain a double blessing; blessings for you, and blessings for the nation.

APPLICATION

Since America's blessings are tied to the people of our great nation obeying God's commandments, today, pray for your country, for your leaders, and for the elections this year. Ask God to forgive our nation for not following his ways. Petition God to install leaders who've put their faith in Jesus and desire to lead our nation in a manner that would please him and bring him glory.

PRAYER

Dear God, please forgive us and our nation for we have greatly sinned against you! How far we have fallen from our former glory when our founders came here to fulfill your Great Commission. I pray that you guide our president and other national, state, and local leaders in the decisions they make and the direction in which they lead us, the people. I also pray that you help all of those leaders know you and put their faith in Jesus. You know there's a big election coming up. Please help people vote this year. Please ensure the voting is accurate and not tampered with or fraudulent. I pray that you help each of us vote for the candidates you're backing that will lead our city, state, and nation as you would lead it. I hope that you continue to smile on our great nation.

Thanks for reading this devotional. If you'd like to show your support for my work, please leave a review wherever you purchased this book. It's free to do, and it'll only take you a minute to write a quick sentence expressing your thoughts about the book. Your review is very important to independent, self-published authors like me. Internet and online bookstore algorithms favor books with reviews. They display in search results and at the top of search results more often than books without reviews. I even need a minimum number of reviews before I can purchase certain advertising. So, your review will help more people find this book. That will in turn help me sell more books, which means I can keep writing books for you. Go to rapture911.com/reviews if you need a link to where you can leave a review.

Thanks for your support!

Marsha

READ
RAPTURE 911:
WHAT TO DO IF YOU'RE LEFT BEHIND

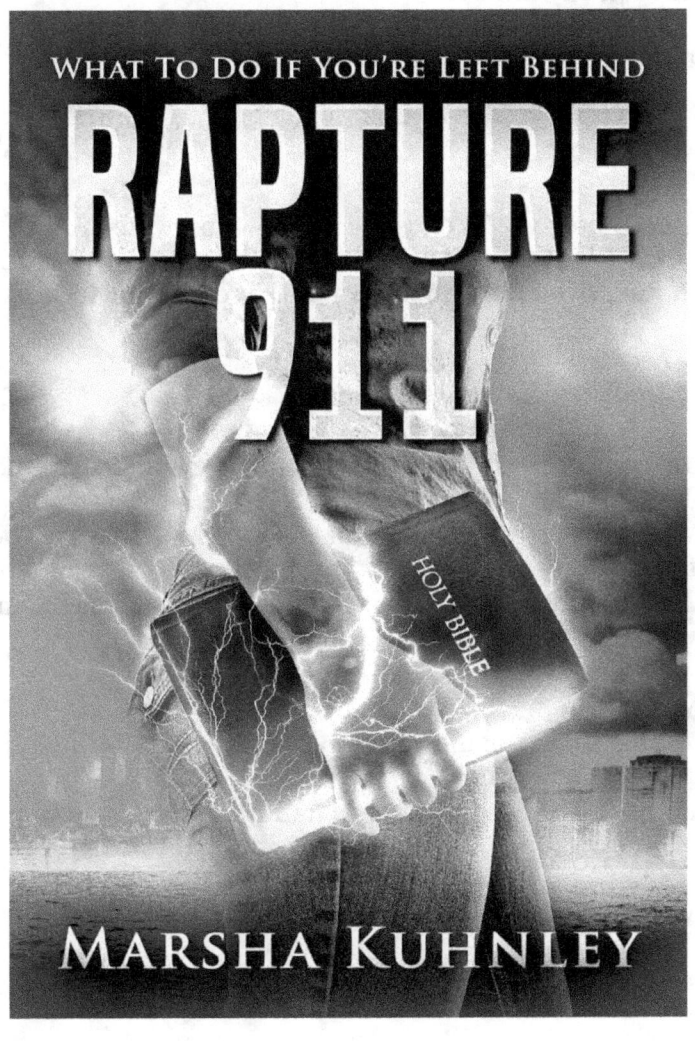

The End of the World is coming...

...but it's not what Hollywood portrays.

Are you uncertain about what God has in store for humanity? Do you fear for the salvation of your family and friends?

It could happen any minute.

The Rapture.

Will you be Left Behind to survive the Apocalypse? You can join the millions who will be saved.

Do you already believe? Then you can help those who are Left Behind. *Rapture 911: What To Do If You're Left Behind* is your all-in-one resource to survive the Tribulation and prepare for Jesus's Second Coming.

Inside this book is the following:
- Easy-to-understand Biblical analysis.
- Theological overview of forthcoming events surrounding the End Times.
- Why millions of people will disappear and what those Left Behind can do to be saved.
- The truth behind fake news and deceptions surfacing today that will be prominent after the Rapture.
- Examples of prophecies fulfilled that prove God's Word is trustworthy.
- Coping mechanisms from Biblical heroes to better handle shame, grief, and fear.
- A checklist of preparations, a handy glossary, and much, much more!

You'll love this handbook for navigating the Last Days because you want to live in Heaven and you care about saving your loved one's souls.

Get it now.

BOOKS BY MARSHA KUHNLEY

Rapture 911 Series
*Rapture 911: What To Do If You're Left Behind
Rapture 911: What To Do If You're Left Behind (Pocket Edition)
Rapture 911: 10 Day Devotional
Rapture 911: Prophecy Reference Bible

End Times Armor Series
The Election Omen: Your Vote Matters
The Election Omen: 10 Day Devotional

Other Works
Seeing The Light In Dark Times: 10 Day Devotional

Visit Marsha's website to find these books
rapture911.com

* - Also available as an audiobook

ABOUT THE AUTHOR

Marsha Kuhnley is an American author of Christian non-fiction books. She has a passion for Bible prophecy, finance, and economics. She received her MBA in Finance and BA in Economics from the University of New Mexico. Prior to becoming an author, she enjoyed a career at Intel Corporation. She uses her education and career experience to take complex Biblical information and present it in easily understandable concepts. You'll benefit from over a decade of her research and study of the Bible, Bible prophecy, and Rapture theology. She lives in Albuquerque, NM with her husband where they attend Calvary Church.

CONNECT WITH MARSHA

rapture911.com/connect

ENDNOTES

[1] "The Mayflower Compact," National Center, https://nationalcenter.org/MayflowerCompact.html, accessed April 14, 2020.

[2] "Declaration of Independence," National Archives, https://www.archives.gov/founding-docs/declaration-transcript, accessed April 14, 2020.

[3] "Washington's Inaugural Address of 1789," National Archives, https://www.archives.gov/exhibits/american_originals/inaugtxt.html, accessed April 14, 2020.